101 TERRIBLE RECORD SLEEVES
MICHAEL SUMNER

100% PURE NAFF

Copyright © Michael Sumner 2023. All rights reserved.

This book or any portion thereof may not be reproduced or used in any manner whatsoever without the express written permission of the publisher except for the use of brief quotations in a book review.

Strenuous attempts have been made to credit all copyrighted materials used in this book. All such materials and trademarks, which are referenced in this book, are the full property of their respective copyright owners. Every effort has been made to obtain copyright permission for material quoted in this book. Any omissions will be rectified in future editions.

Cover image by: Michael Shepherd
Book design by: SWATT Books Ltd

ISBN: 978-1-7394537-0-1(Hardback)

Printed in the United Kingdom
First Printing, 2023

FOREWORD

What would drive somebody to travel the globe, hunting for the worst examples of art and design ever committed to record sleeves? All those hours spent in sweltering antiques shops in India, dusty shop basements in darkest Lithuania and 5am starts on freezing mornings at Croatian flea markets. Well the truth is, I was primarily (or at least at the start) looking for good records. That is, rare records. Records that collectors would pay a pretty penny for.

Part of the job of a record dealer is searching through piles and piles of worthless records in search of a gem. This is often a fruitless task, but I began to start buying awful record sleeves along the way that would amuse me and my chums. This meant that if I spent all day ploughing through charity shops for something of worth and was unsuccessful (as is usually the case), then at least I had something to show for it if I found a real turkey. And then as my collection of terrible sleeves began to grow, the idea of a book grew. So now I began to really kill two birds with one stone, by searching for both the best and the worst of records at the same time. Bingo. Like Cadbury's Flake, a successful by-product may have been unearthed out of the stuff destined for the bin.

And it has been undeniably fun, from the places visited and characters met en route, to the thrill of finding something truly awful and onto researching the back stories of some of these wonderful chancers. So hats off to the underdog, may they breathe again. And remember, if you can't be a huge success in life, be a magnificent failure!

THE SPOTNICKS:
OUT-A SPACE THE SPOTNICKS IN LONDON

"'Ello, 'ello, 'ello, what's going on 'ere then? Under the Roads and Highways Act 1948, section 12c, it is prohibited to land a space rocket on the pavement thereby obstructing pedestrians. Shift this spacecraft before I issue a fixed penalty, carrying a fine of 6 shillings. Please launch and land in more suitable environs, such as the moon or Mars. Off you trot lads. And wipe that smirk off your face, Tinkerbell, before I run you up the station."

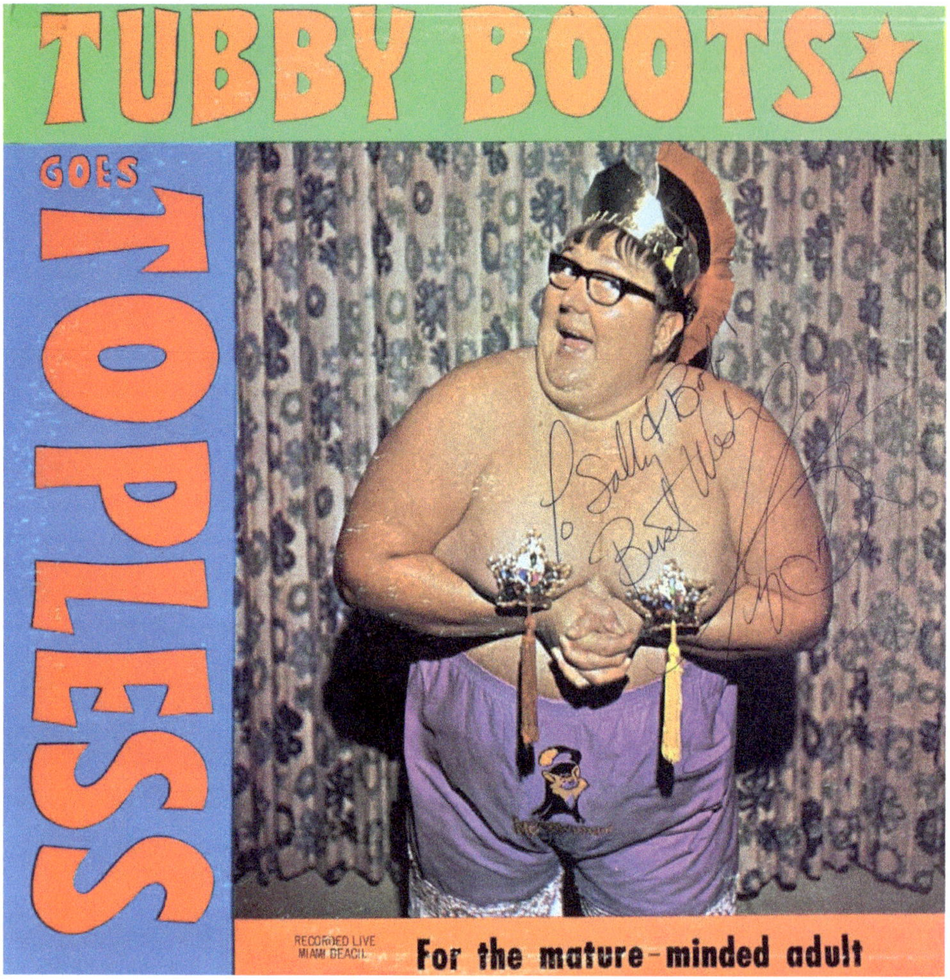

TUBBY BOOTS:
THIN MAY BE IN – BUT FAT'S WHERE IT'S AT

American entertainer Charles 'Tubby' Booth took his 375 pounds and moobs*, and made a career out of it. With albums such as Thin May Be In – But Fat's Where It's At and Songs For Swingers. Tubby's routine included attaching pasties to his tits and swinging them about simultaneously in opposite directions. His 'work' took him to performing in nightclubs, carnival shows, strip joints and finally to low-rent motel lounges in his later years.

As they say in the States, if life gives you lemons, make lemonade.

*Man boobs

JAMES LAST:
OP KLOMPEN

The scourge of all record dealers is the James Last album, or should I say the million James Last albums, junking up attics, flea markets and charity shops all over Europe. Estimated to have sold over 200 million copies of the bloody things; it is said that at his peak, Herr Last was knocking out a new album every week.

The record dealer's fear of driving miles to buy a potentially great record collection, only to find a case full of Last's albums, led to an advert for 'Records Wanted' in my local paper ending with the line 'NO JAMES LAST ALBUMS'. Being singled out like that is no pretty mean achievement. But ultimately, the joke is on us. He must have made a fortune. No wonder he looks so bloody smug in his clogs and daft trousers.

JOHNNY GUITAR WATSON: A REAL MOTHER

Ever the flamboyant showman, superfly JGW poses in his pimped-up pram for his 1970 funk album stonker 'A Real Mother'. That's what real mothers do, you see. Note the personalised number plate, bonnet badge and guitar carved into the panels. Real mothers then get one of their cash-strapped gals a job as a lackey to push them around the local park all day.

QUARTERFLASH:
TAKE ANOTHER PICTURE

I must confess, mannequins, puppets and ventriloquist's dolls give me the willies. Check out the terrifying Hugo in the 1945 film Dead Of Night, or Talky Tina in The Twilight Zone episode Living Doll to see why. Then imagine waking up to one of these at the end of the bed in the middle of the night. The demonic doll is staring at you impassively, before manically uttering the spine-chilling line 'CAN I BE YOUR SPECIAL FRIEND???!!!'

WATERLOO & ROBINSON:
UNSERE LIEDER

I wonder if these two chuckle bunnies spend their afternoons practising their synchronised dance moves. I bet they go shopping together as well. Bless.

RUSTY GOFFE:
FOR YOUR ENTERTAINMENT

Not only does Rusty play organ, guitar, bagpipes, trumpet, post horn, timpani, gong, side drum, cymbals and tubular bells, but he also played an Oompa-Lompa in Willy Wonka & The Chocolate Factory, a Jawa in Star Wars and had a small role in Flash Gordon. Is there no end to his talents?

And in order to emphasise Rusty's Unique Selling Point further, he has been made to look as small as possible on the sleeve. So small, in fact, that he can sit quite happily on a musical note, content in the knowledge that he has more talent in his little finger than the rest of us put together.

CERRONE: SUPERNATURE

The creepiest aspect of this sleeve isn't the animal headed humans or corpse on the operating table, but the menacing feral monkey-boy in flares. He goes by the name of Cerrone, produced some of the greatest disco music known to man, and looks like he is ready to pounce on you and gorge on your still beating heart.

STAG:
BLACK BETTY

One for the lay-dees.

This reminds one of those tacky Chippendale stripper's calendars hanging in housewives' kitchens in Wakefield council estates circa 1984. I suppose it was only a matter of time though before the women caught up with all the Sam Fox posters and Razzle centre-folds pinned up in factories, garages and workplaces around the UK at the time.

German poodle smooth synth-pop at its worst.

FRITZ FETZER
PETRA PILZ

This badass guitar playing chick magnet, aka Little Lord, is on top of my party invite list every time.

KAREL VAGNER:
JAMBO KARLA VAGNERA

As was said about the late maverick snooker player Alex Higgins, Karel Vagner looks like a man who has seen trouble. Like the favourite wayward uncle who never settled down, Karel looks like he spent his days under Communist rule importing knock-off fake leather jackets and bad aftershave from his mate Boris in Belarus.

Karel has such big dick energy that he can rock up to the photo-shoot for his new album in his street hustling togs, and nobody dares say a thing. He is wearing similar clothes and aftershave to the gear he is going to sell you after the shoot, straight from the boot of his Skoda.

#12

THE VETERANS:
I'M JOGGING

Belgium's own Chuckle Brothers, Gus Roan and Marc Malyster, released this single in 1980 to cash in on the jogging fad hitting the country. And if you think this sleeve is bad, check out the video.

Surrounded by scantily clad Benny Hill's Angel-esque dolly birds, Roan wheezes and pervs about to an irritating ditty that will plant a worm in your ear all day.

This song would be too naff even for the Eurovision Song Contests. Nil Points would be too generous.

ALVIN LEE:
RX5

What would Beavis and Butthead make of this?

"Hey dude, I always thought C3PO was a bit, like, y'know, lame and stuff, but he can totally rock out."

"Totally dude. We just need R2D2 on drums."

"That'd be awesome."

ARGENTINA CORAL:
CANTE GITANO

It's the mouth that does it. Cruel and masculine. Señora Coral will handcuff you to the bed naked, rob you of your valuables and set the house on fire on the way out as a parting shot. Get the hell outta there while you can, bro.

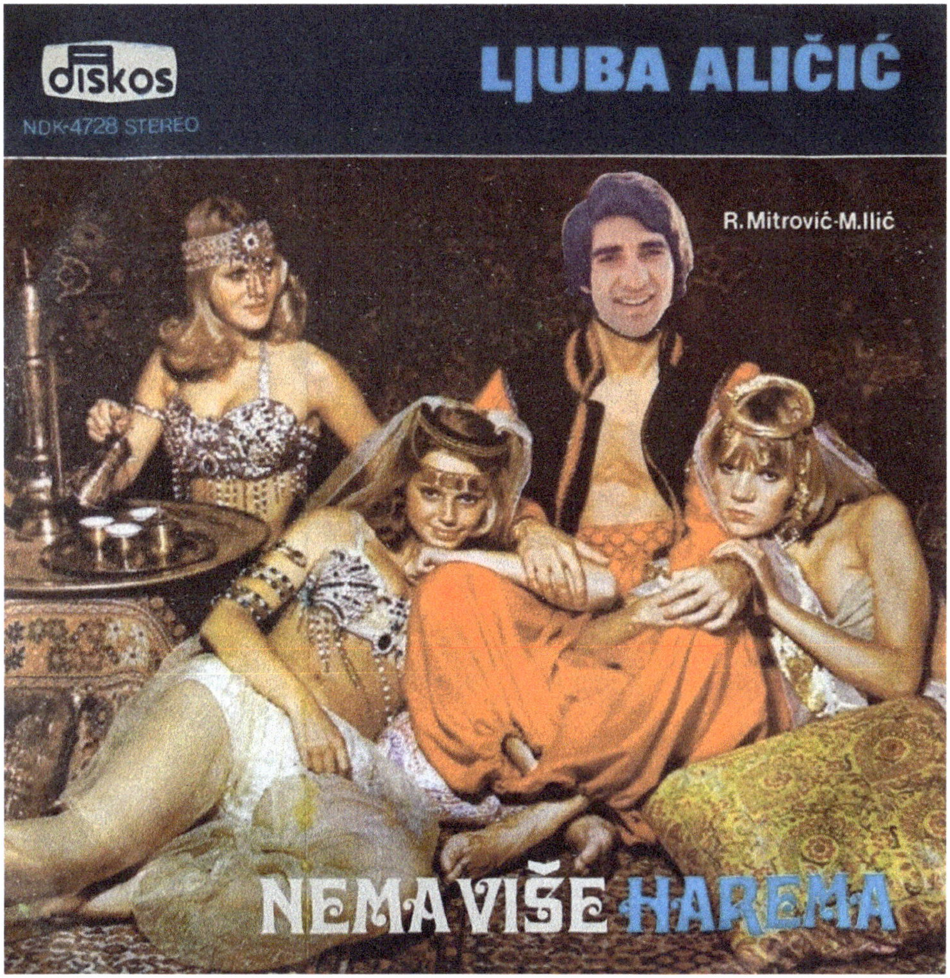

LJUBA ALIČIĆ:
NEMA VIŠE HAREMA (NO MORE HAREMS)

Serbian Romani folk singer Ljuba had a big hit with 'Ciganin sam, al' najlepši'. It translates roughly as, 'I am a gypsy, but the most beautiful', so humility clearly wasn't his forte. So how do you give off the impression that your Roma virility and riches have afforded you a life of untold luxury?

Simple. Just cut out a photo of your head and glue it to an old picture of a prince surrounded by a harem of beauties. Nobody will notice and that'll show 'em. Job done.

WENCHIN: SELF-TITLED

Ye Gods! Robert Wegrzyn's solo outing sees himself on top of a flame snorting, shimmering white horse, with a magnificent bird of prey on his shoulder. His gang of not-so-merry hanger-ons resemble a bunch of twizzle bearded, bespectacled 1970s social science lecturers, kind of out of time and place in this Tolkienesque world.

The topless hirsute men and stroppy looking woman in front look like they would hardly strike fear into the mythical creatures of the night. Granted, the woman at the front does look quite angry, in a huffy sort of way. But this is in a more, 'I'm very cross with you, Mr Dragon, for burning down our villages' manner.

BONED:
UP AT THE CRACK

Altogether now…

"Is that a guitar in your pants, or are you just pleased to see me?" etc, etc.

HEINO:
SELF-TITLED

Whether churning out syrupy sweet pop melodies or slightly worrying songs about the mountains, trees and valleys of the Fatherland, Heino has been the Schlager-meister general of German popular music for decades.

Seeing his trademark bleached blonde hair and dark glasses on TV for years, along with the consistent level of atrocious music, must have been like comfort food to Germans. You know it's not good, but it makes you feel safe.

He reminds me of a Euro-Andy Warhol, or the Finnish musician Jimi Tenor, which is a kinda cool look. But this is Heino, remember. And the poodles just make matters worse.

STEELOVER:
GLOVE ME

This was the Belgian heavy metal outfit's only album, thank God, and brings to mind Spinal Tap's piss-take song 'Smell The Glove'. This is where art and satire become blurred somewhat, especially considering this album came out in 1984, the same year as the film This Is Spinal Tap.

I found this shocker in the bottom of a dusty box whilst perusing a Polish junk shop, and wondered whether I'd done the right thing by unleashing this horror upon humanity from its resting place. Should I have let this hell-hound lie? Not opened Pandora's Box? Left the puzzle box from the Hellraiser film at the Moroccan market? Of course not! Dog's breath sleeves like this should be celebrated in all their awfulness. But there will be casualties.

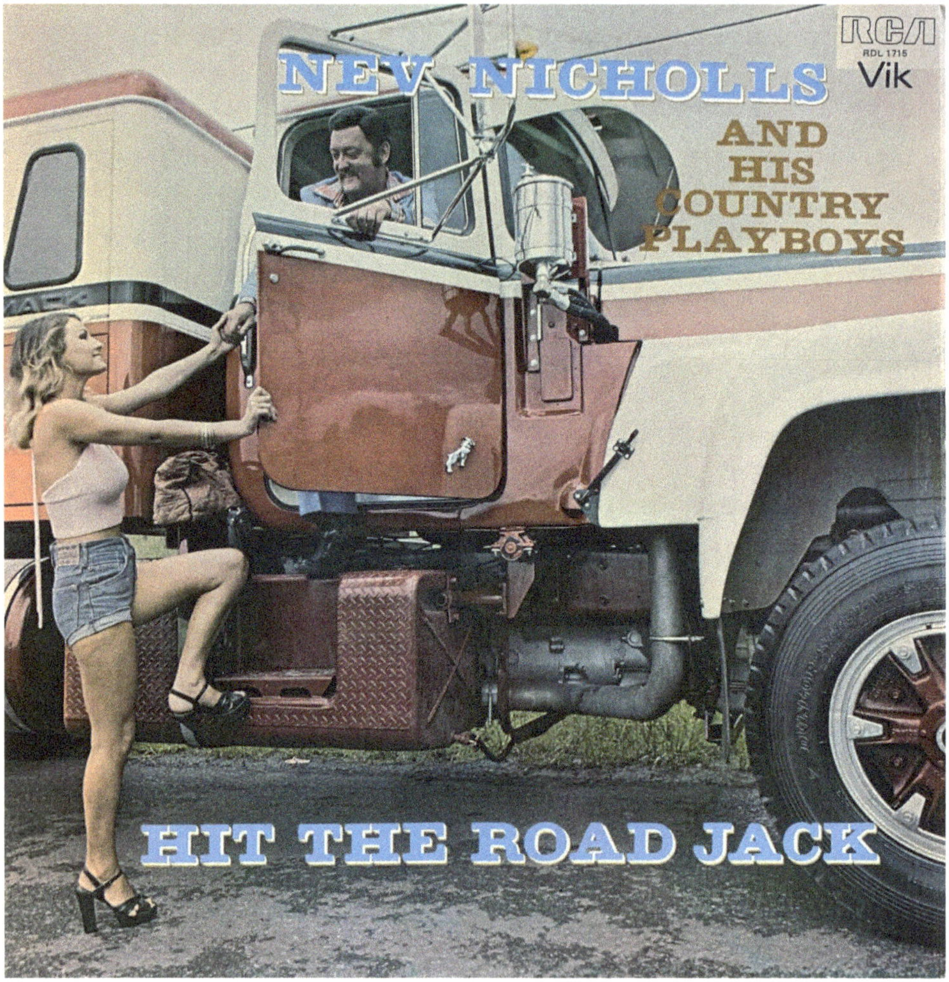

NEV NICHOLLS AND HIS COUNTRY PLAYBOYS: HIT THE ROAD JACK

"Once the rig is parked up and the piss bottles emptied in a nearby hedge after a hard day's hauling across the Midwest, it's time for a trip to Sloppy Joe's greasy cafe. Hunger satisfied, gotta catch up with the boys at the tavern for a cold Miller, where we compare the Daisy Duke-looking hookers we picked up en route for a ride."

Keep on truckin', mother truckers.

FRED EMNEY: SELF-TITLED

Comedian and actor Fred Emney carved out a career principally playing fat toffs, but he also appeared in the kids' show Pinky and Perky and had a small role playing an old xenophobe in The Italian Job.

Looking like a sadistic teacher, that monocled glare will give anybody of a certain age cold sweats as they relive those British school days of yore. I'm having flashbacks myself of the dreaded music lessons and those awful, joyless morning assemblies.

Oh, The Horror! The Horror!

MIJA ALEKSIĆ:
SEKS I KEKS (SEX AND BISCUITS)

- "Hey my friend, have you got any nudey pictures of your wife?"

- "No, I haven't!"

- "Wanna buy some?"

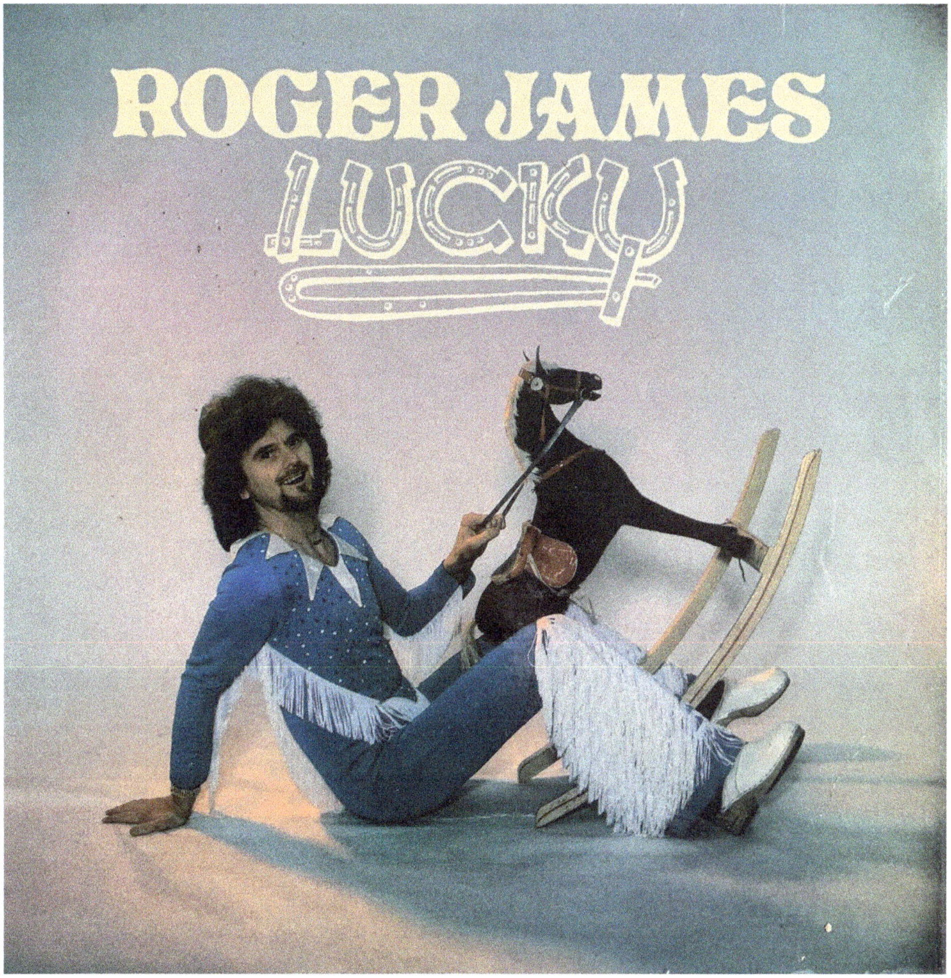

ROGER JAMES: LUCKY

The disconnect between how Roger James originally envisaged his sleeve, and the reality of what he actually ended up with, is both palpable and painful. Instead of sitting atop a beautiful palomino horse and looking coolly into the distance, before riding off into the sunset like the Malboro Man, time and money constraints dictated otherwise. Fate played its cruel card, and calling the album Lucky only twists the knife deeper.

He looks the optimistic type though. The sort of chap who gets straight back on his (rocking) horse if he falls off.

SANDY BARON'S GOD SAVE THE QUEENS

Sandy Baron's 1972 gay comedy album was composed of a number of dialogues between the straight and gay communities in an attempt to break down homosexual stereotypes.

So why put a flamboyant mincing 'queen' on the sleeve, surrounded by over chummy bunnies, birds, butterflies and Bambi, thus being guilty of the very thing he was calling out? But it was 1972, so let's not be too harsh on him, although some quarters of the gay community called him out for trying to capitalise on their cause.

Sandy Baron was straight, by the way.

THE FABULOUS FONTANAS:
IF YOU'RE IRISH COME INTO THE PARLOUR

These not-so-chirpy paddies look like they could turn nasty after one too many Guinnesses. They may as well have named this album 'If You Are English, Stay Out Of Our Boozer If You Know What's Good For You'.

DAISY DAZE AND THE BUMBLE BEES: PLANET O

"We are pirates from the Planet 0, We'll enslave you, We will break your soul", begins this bizarre tune about lusty alien swashbucklers, reminiscent of the song 'Future Sailor' from the comedy Mighty Boosh.

Ed Wood's 1954 film, Plan B From Outer Space is often cited as the worst film ever made, and this has to be the pop equivalent of sci-fi naff. And why is the damsel in distress in a compromising position *'sans culottes'*?

At least the Dr Manhattan/alien dude isn't "going commando", donning a pair of shiny blue alien speedos to protect his modesty – the only evidence of any shred of decency about this whole sordid affair.

VARIOUS ARTISTS:
TOP SZENE HAMBURG

The worst thing about this revolting but ingenious sleeve for a German Schlager compilation is that it came with a huge poster with the same image. Forget upsetting your parents as a teenager by blu-tacking a Sex Pistols 'Never Mind The Bollocks' poster up in your bedroom. A Top Szene Hamburg poster on your wall would really convince the old squares that you are one sick puppy.

GERHARD POLT:
LEBERKÄS› HAWAII

If you are one of those foodie types who think Hawaiian pizza is a bit naff, this will make you weep into your sourdough zayt and za'atar crackers. Liver cheese and pineapple, served on a bed of wilted lettuce, with a superimposed Bavarian actor's head on top. German cuisine has never looked so *ungeniessbar*.

BRIAN MAXINE

BRIAN MAXINE: KING OF THE RING

Our Brian was a professional wrestler in the late 60s/early 70s, swanning around the ring in his regal attire and then tossing his opponents about on his way to winning both the British Welterweight and Middleweight Championships.

But his talents and self-promotion didn't end there. He was also a budding Country & Western singer, so why not combine the two for the sleeve of his first album? He did perform on occasion with legendary folk group Fairport Convention though, so kudos to Brian there.

QUIM BARREIROS:
RECEBI UM CONVITE (À CASA DA JÓQUINA)

Blimey. This little find certainly ticks all the boxes.

With a naked Portuguese Borat look-alike playing the accordion over his privates, this sleeve is like breaking wind in a lift. It is wrong on so many levels. Let's hope he doesn't have an accident when he pushes those bellows together.

All he needs now is an amusing name that translates into some vulgar slang for a female's 'unmentionables'. Oh, hold on a minute...

BANJO BAND IVANA MLADKA:
NASHLEDANOU!

I almost missed this innocuous looking sleeve, but my keen nose for sleeves that are 'not-rights' smelled a rat. And that rat was the matey in the middle who managed to supersize his head to make him stand out from the rest of the band. Was this down to ego? Were the others aware at the time, or was foul play down at the printers at work? Or does his cheesy grin suggest a more mischievous side? The plot thickens.

Or, of course, he may just have an unfeasibly big head.

Suggestions on a postcard to the usual address please.

RIO:
SEX CRIMES

With tracks such as 'Pay For Love', 'Dirty Movies' and 'Danger Zone', Rio probably knew deep down they would not become the new Black Sabbath. So how did they attempt to shift a lame product to an impressionable teenage market?

By cramming in as many bad rock clichés as possible onto one sleeve, that's how.

Rio didn't sprinkle glitter gently upon a shit sandwich of songs with a decent sleeve. Instead, they pulled up mob-handed in a dumper truck, and unloaded a huge pile of manure onto that turd of a record. Actually, that's pretty rock and roll.

OLYMPIC:
LABORATOŘ

Prague rock band Olympic have been knocking around since 1962, with this album being released in 1982 whilst the Czech Republic was still under communist rule. Like some fourth division Kraftwerk album sleeve, this unglamorous vision of drab housing, crappy Skoda* cars and lifeless dummies in colourless clothing gives us a bleak snapshot of life under the totalitarian regime.

Actually, it's pretty cool in a Commie chic sort of way.

*Skoda means 'Too bad!' in Czech

A CONCERT BY THE METROPOLITAN POLICE BAND AND CHOIR

Imagine being awakened at 5am by a loud and insistent banging on the door, and being confronted by this scene of authoritarian fear and loathing.

Imagine then thinking this frightening image would endear the public to purchase an album by the Met's own band and choir. An opportunity to showcase both the rozzers' musical talents and a more human side to policing, was lost on this lot.

In future, stick to hitting people on the head with truncheons please. Leave the music to the hippies. We know where we stand that way. And we promise in return to not let the hippies join the Met.

![Klik-Klak record cover - Miljuš Svetlana - Bračna veza teža od poreza]

MILJUŠ SVETLANA:
BRAČNA VEZA TEŽA OD POREZA (MARITAL RELATIONSHIP TAX THESIS)

"Hey Big Boy, you gonna come up and see me some time soon? A girl can get awful lonesome round here swinging on ma klikety klaks. Play yer cards right and I'll swing *your* klik klacks honey, then bury your face in my jungle pits, you fuzzy little man peach."

TOZOVAC:
JEREMIJA

Folk singer and TV personality Tozovac's womanising ways are legendary*, and what better way to show one's power and virility by dressing up as a caped dictator with a powerful weapon erect between his legs. Tozovac looks prepared for action - primed and ready to fire off a few rounds on his unsuspecting victims.

*In Serbia, anyway.

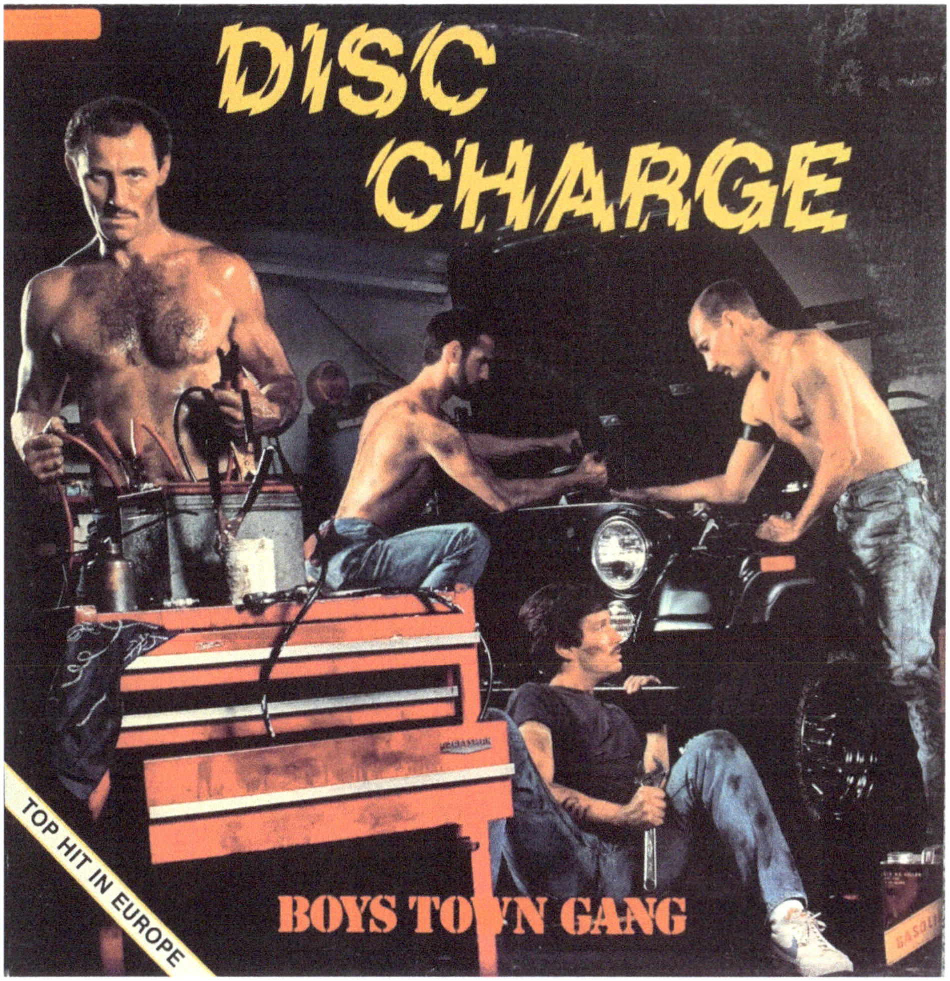

BOYS TOWN GANG:
DISC CHARGE

It's sure getting hot and sweaty down in the garage today with these moustachioed mechanics, so much so that they have to take their tops off as they work their spanners hard. Don't let the fact that they are from San Francisco, play disco, and one of the boys has a leather arm band fool you. They are 100% Men's Men.

SUE BARNETT:
FIT FOR LIFE! WITH SUE BARNETT

This reminds me of your auntie who always drinks too much at family gatherings and gets down on the kitchen floor claiming, "I may be 43, but I can still do the splits."

Or in my case, drinking too much at family gatherings and getting down on the kitchen floor and break dancing. I've since stopped doing this after 'doing a mischief' and suffering a dislocated index finger on the last attempt. I was 43.

There is a moral to this story for all over 40s. If you're tempted to show the kids that you've still got it, just remember you haven't. You look like Sue Barnett.

PASSPORT: LOOKING THRU

Hipgnosis was a UK based art collective behind some of the most iconic album sleeves of the 1960s and 70s. The creative likes of Storm Thorgerson and Aubrey Powell were responsible for the wonderful psychedelic sleeves of bands such as Pink Floyd, Yes and Peter Gabriel. They were not, however, responsible for this garish, pseudo intelligent design that leaves one feeling slightly queasy, or even sea sick.

Having seen this, Thorgerson and Powell would have taken their foot right off the creative pedal and had a few weeks holiday in Spain. They would have smiled quietly to themselves as they sipped a cold Estrella on the beach, thinking about the laughable quality of the competition snapping at their heels upon their return to work.

HEINZ ZABEL:
AUF GROSSER FAHRT

Mein Gott. Das für ein Horror! This looks like some Hitler Youth party out for a healthy march in the Bavarian countryside, playing traditional Teutonic folk songs, accompanied by guitar and loud farting. I assume that's what Auf Grosser Fahrt means.

RICKY SKAGGS:
LOVE'S GONNA GET YA!

Lock up your daughters, Kentuckian country star and love machine Ricky Skaggs is on the prowl! Beautifully coiffed, with pressed denims, shiny heels a-tapping away and sleeves nonchalantly rolled up, Ricky is ready for love.

No really. Lock up your daughters.

KEEP IT GAY:
CONVERSATIONAL MUSIC

Date with a hot chick?
Keep it gay.

Engaging in some light chit chat, amuse-bouches and witty repartee?
Keep it gay.

Organ stylings?
Keep it gay.

CAPT. SKY:
CONCERNED PARTY NO 1

Looking like a reject extra from the film Flash Gordon, Captain Sky (real name Daryl Cameron) was part of the P-Funk movement, which combined futuristic imagery with psychedelic funk. As the costumes, stage acts and all-round weirdness of such acts like Capt. Sky, Funkadelic and Parliament hit cosmic levels, P-Funk eventually bombed. Basically, mainstream black audiences were too freaked out, man, and disco was where it was at.

I blame it on the copious amounts of acid. But what a trip.

#44

ANIMAL KWACKERS: SELF-TITLED

I loved the Animal Kwackers. A blatant bootleg rip-off of the more polished American kids' show The Banana Splits, the Kwackers covered popular rock and pop songs. They had Bingo, we had Bongo. They had shiny outfits and biffed about on cool motorised go-karts with cheesy grins. All the Kwackers had were some manky old hand-me-down animal suits out of some trunk in the attic of Yorkshire TV. Northern thrift and low budgets in Yorkshire could never compete with their rivals over the pond in California, where everything is bigger and brighter.

And Kwacker's drummer Geoff Nicholls played in Black Sabbath. So yeah, I'm Team Kwackers all the way. The Banana Splits can go whistle.

JOHNNY HANDLE:
SHE'S A BIG LASS, SHE'S A BONNY LASS

The burning head scratch here is two-fold, the obvious being Johnny Handle's title of choice. What is more puzzling though is how he hoodwinked 'our lass' to appear on the sleeve. Judging by her slightly awkward expression, one can imagine she took some persuading. Meanwhile, Johnny is looking quite pleased with himself.

You could of course argue that Geordie Johnny is supporting more curvaceous women in a society obsessed with size 8's. But bearing in mind this was the 1970s, and with that smirk on his face, Johnny Handle is found guilty by this kangaroo court.

THE FIDGETY FEET JAZZBAND:
STONED

This elusive band obviously liked a sherbet and a biff or two, so much so that it may have derailed their music ambitions. There is so little to go on. We can't even see their faces.

Like Sir Winston Churchill's comments about the role of the Soviet Union in WWII, The Fidgety Feet Jazzband 'is a riddle wrapped in a mystery inside an enigma'. Long may it remain that way as sometimes, less is more.

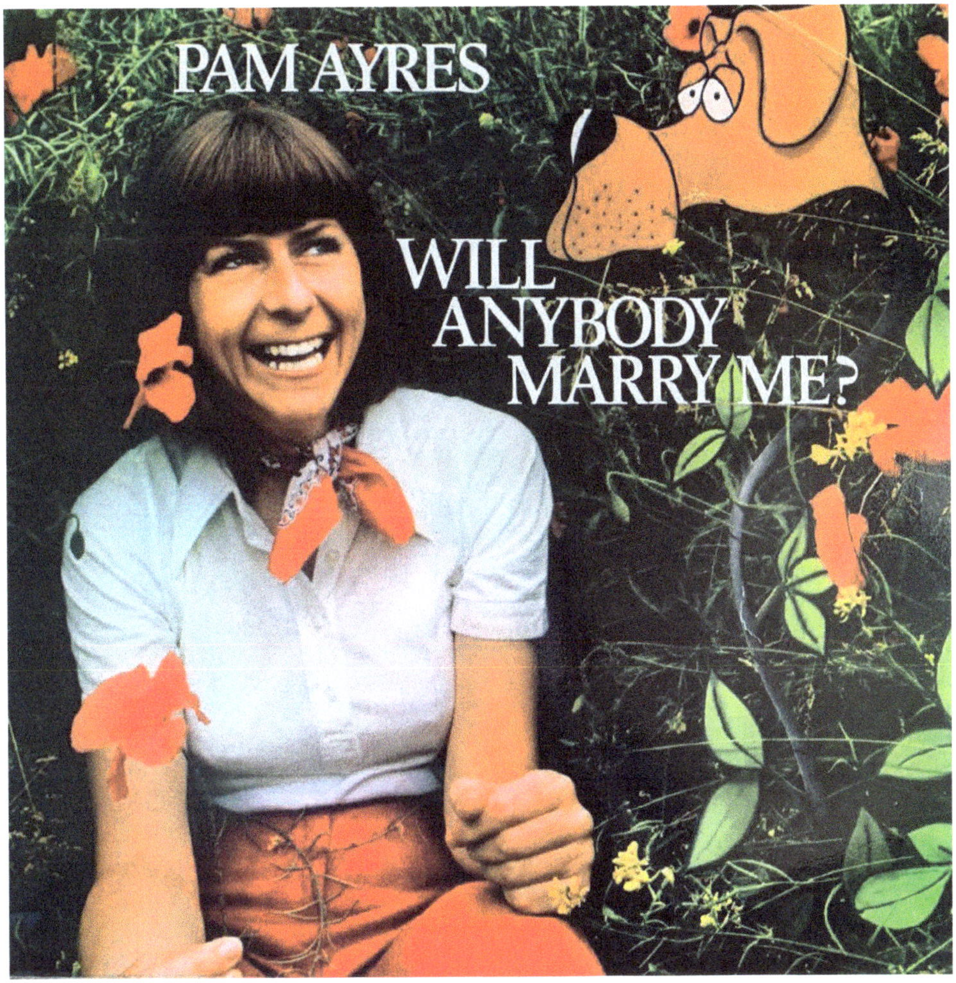

PAM AYRES:
WILL ANYBODY MARRY ME?

Self-pity is probably the worst pheromone of all to wear when attracting a mate. Or maybe it is an early example of the humblebrag. She looks alright to me, but perhaps slightly unhinged. It's that over-chummy doey-eyed hang dog that gives this sleeve Grade D-.

VARIOUS:
WHERE ARE THE DEAD?

There are scores of religious albums to be found in American thrift stores, either from Christian singing families, or preachers committing their sermons to vinyl to reach a larger audience. Or in the latter's case, to line their pockets as well. This may come across as a tad cynical, but preaching in the States is BIG business.

This particular example is a right jolly old gloom-fest. The sleeve proclaims to have the answer to the Big Question etched into the wax. Not a bad sales pitch for just $10, available from recommended retail stores, of course.

R-GO:
AMULETT

KERR-POW!!

What's going on here, then? Hungarian pop rockers R-GO go for the Bollywood adventure film poster look, complete with handsome hero, dusky maiden, karate chopping bad guy and a mildly cross-eyed leopard set in some exotic desert location where the sun burns white hot.

Which still doesn't answer the question, what's going on here, then? Why?

CLINKERS:
THE FIRST CLINKERS

The most offensive thing about this incredibly rare private pressing isn't the bloke taking a dump in a bed pan with an image of the Sussex folky band looking up his nipsy on it. It's that one of the tracks on the album is called 'The Great Poofter'.

There was never a 'Second Clinkers' album as far as we know. I wonder why.

UDO LINDENBERG & DAS PANIK-ORCHESTER: SISTER KING KONG

When I called in on my Uncle Jim unaware once, he was sitting in front of the telly in his underpants, spread-eagled, 'airing his legs'. According to scientists, this is now known as 'manspreading'.

This is acceptable in my retired uncle's case, sitting in the comfort of his home, watching his favourite TV show 'Walker, Texas Ranger'. In fact, it is to be championed. He deserves it.

However, it is seen as bad form to spread in public these days, for example, on a tube journey or in the doctor's waiting room. But to proudly splay one's sweaty gusset on your latest album cover, with references to King Kong, is beyond the pale, Udo. Turn it in, mate.

BLACK LACE: AGADOO

Anyone in the UK over 40 will remember this pair, prancing about like a couple of tits, with their 'party anthems' such as 'Agadoo' (TOP-HIT ENGLAND), 'Do The Conga' and 'Gang Band'. And we pranced about like tits with them, to our chagrin now.

On a holiday camp near Skegness in the 80s, they were playing live and my sister had her photo taken with them after the show.

She was so proud at the time.

ŽENY:
K SMRTI VYLEKÁN

-"Hi guys, I've got a great idea for our new album sleeve… We all strip off butt naked except for our socks!"
-'Er, ok, but we don't want everyone to see our todgers."
-"We'll just tuck them in under the bridges, and it will look fine."
-"Well ok, if you are sure… "

The album title translates as 'Scared to Death', which is how I felt when I purchased this off a big no-nonsense looking gypsy in a stained white vest at a Prague flea market. He eyed me suspiciously when this Englishman made his strange purchase.

BILLY COBHAM – GEORGE DUKE BAND: 'LIVE' ON TOUR IN EUROPE

Billy may have the biggest chops in the drumming stratosphere, and Georgie is no slouch either, but they lost it big time with this moment of madness. What were they thinking?

The image of these two jazz legends creeping-and-a-crawling around Europe on their digits reminds me of those possessed hands in Evil Dead 2.

File under 'So bad it's good'.

WILD OATES: SELF-TITLED

Who are these fez wearing trick-asses? Wild Oates were a comedy/vaudeville act on the northern club scene, belting out butchered covers of classic songs to boozed up locals on a Saturday night. They certainly look like they should be auditioning for Phoenix Nights.

The little fella is Big Mick, who not only drummed but played Trumpkin in Prince Caspian, Jack Large in Blackadder, Grumbly in Psychoville and a cross dresser in Lexx. He also looks rather fetching on the cover of their second and final album, wearing high heels, a blonde wig and a pretty pink frock. If that's what you're into, of course.

PLEASE:
MANILA THRILLER

If the devil has all the best tunes, he must also take responsibility for the worst sleeves. Yes, we're looking at you, Please.

This is actually a great hidden gem of an album by the Filipino Funksters. But with the six band members identically dressed in boxing attire, staging a pagga in the shower no less, the record was never going to win any design awards on the sleeve front. They got da funk, for sure, but basing an album sleeve around the fact that Manila rhymes with Thriller and it links to boxing, is their bad.

Maybe that's why they are duffing each other up, blaming one another for the sleeve.

BOLLARDS:
BOLLARDS!

Can you imagine growing up on the same council estate as this bunch of roughs, tear-arsing about on their dirt bikes? Maybe you did. Released on the West Country label Bumpkin, it followed in the same salacious vein as label mates Mike Connor and the Carrot Crunchers. As with the number on their bikes, it was given a catalogue number of 69 despite the label only having released 3 records.

And the innuendos didn't end there. With song titles such as 'Sowin' Me Oats' and 'Find Us The Seamen?', this album offers a snapshot of British working class bawdy humour circa 1977 as punk swept the nation. They do remind me of early boot boy era Slade though. It could have been this lot belting out Christmas number ones, wearing hats with mirrors on and selling peanuts on TV ads.

VARIOUS:
OZVĚNY ČESKOSLOVENSKÝCH SPARTAKIÁD

Spartakiads were mass state exercises, held every 5 years during the era of Czechoslovakian communism. These mandatory displays of up to 750,000 gymnasts showed the outside world the strength and beauty of the regime, along with its participants' impressive underarm hair.

TED NUGENT:
WEEKEND WARRIORS

Good old Ted Nugent.

Gun rights' activist, opponent of animal rights and supporter of 'doing a Nagasaki' on Iraq, Donald Trump is too sissy for Ted. Such is his love of guns (as witnessed on this album sleeve) and dislike of Democrats, it only makes sense that during a concert in 2007, he suggested Obama "suck on my machine gun" whilst flailing assault rifles about.

Seems odd though that a man also known for his homophobic outbursts should choose pink pants and braces as his attire.

KEN GATES:
AS TIME GOES BY

Ken Gates was a rotund American Christian musician with bad taste in denims and a dodgy shirt tucked too tightly into his pants. OK, I get it that Christian music isn't about looking 'cool' and Ken is no Jim Morrison, but come on buddy. Our appearance is still other people's scenery.

Maybe he should have prayed for some spiritual guidance with the album sleeve.

SCORPIONS:
LOVEDRIVE

I suppose this sticky situation is meant to be arty, but it ain't fooling me. He just lost his strawberry Hubba Bubba bubble gum down her cleavage, and is now trying to retrieve it without her noticing before his luck runs out.

LITTLE EVELYN :
LITTLE EVELYN SINGS FOR THE GLORY OF GOD

The wonderful Little Evelyn had infectious enthusiasm, warmth and bags of talent, despite her diminutive 34 inches. According to the notes on the back sleeve, along with her music ministry, Little Evelyn designed and made all her clothes, was a keen ceramist and a comedienne. She also had a miniature stove, sink and refrigerator, but lived in a standard sized house. I've often wondered if fun size Mars Bars make ideal normal size Mars Bars for the vertically challenged?

Anyway, give a big shout out to Little Evelyn. She rocks!

RUDOLF ROKL:
JAK TO CÍTÍM = THE WAY I FEEL IT

A piano reconstructed from old aeroplane parts is quite a novel idea, but I'm only trying to find a positive about this sleeve. On the down side, however, is the scale of the aeroplane parts (the wing looks the same height as our man) and the way it has been hastily superimposed onto the photo with Rudolf's limp wristed hand clumsily pasted on top.

That's The Way I Feel It.

LAID BACK:
PLAY IT STRAIGHT

There's certainly a lot to unpack with this sleeve. Some sort of tropical Wodehousian rannygazoo, I guess. A woman perched precariously on a train (with no track) hurtling towards a vintage motor, whilst a waiter nonchalantly cycles past with drinks balanced on his head. To thicken the plot, a paradise island is visible in the background.

No wait, No, wait! The motorist's head is on fire. Silly me, it all makes sense now.

FELIX SLOVÁČEK, LADISLAV ŠTAIDL SE SVÝM ORCHESTREM: FELIX SLOVÁČEK

Take my hand and I'll transport you to another place, a better place, a place where the sky is blue and there is peace and prosperity for all. The only downside is that I can't guarantee how big or small we'll be when we arrive, which might present a few challenges along the way.

THE RITCHIE FAMILY:
BAD REPUTATION

Village People's disco stablemates The Ritchie Family adopted the same leather 'n' beefcake theme for this cringer. Is that Freddie Mercury prancing in the background in the red wangers?

I remember seeing the Village People on Top Of The Pops as a kid and thinking that there was something a bit odd about them, but I couldn't quite put my finger on it. And was there a fireman in the band?*

*Answer NO. Construction worker, Cop, Cowboy, Indian, GI and leather man, but no fireman.

MICKEY JUPP:
JUPPANESE

Apparently, one way to show your appreciation to the staff at the local Japanese restaurant, upon being presented with your meal, is to make slanty-eyed gestures back at them.

Oh, and that food doesn't even look Japanese anyway. That Oriental food is all the bloody same anyway, eh Mickey boy? Nobody will notice.

And all because Jupp sounds a bit like Jap. Genius.

Triple fail, Mickey boy.

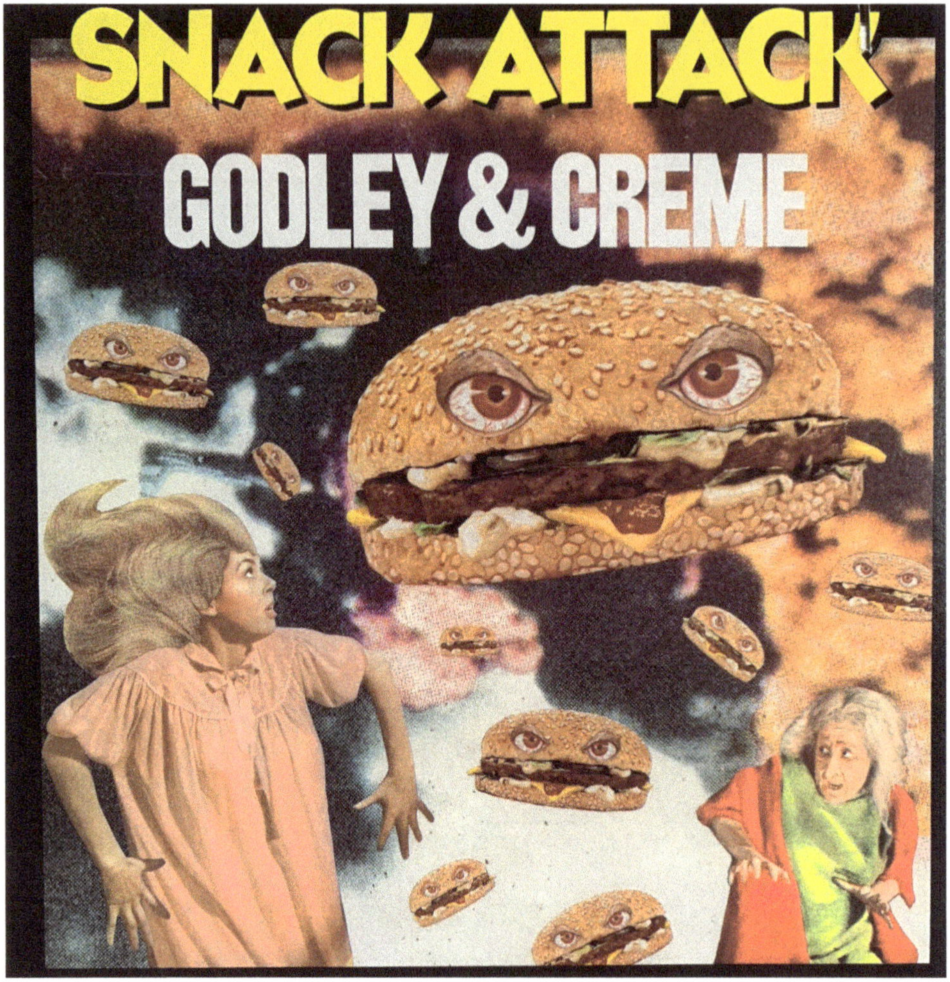

GODLEY & CREME:
SNACK ATTACK

Is this sleeve Godley & Creme's complex metaphor of large fast food conglomerates killing off its customer base with unhealthy snacks? Or is it just a crap sleeve of angry looking flying hamburgers, resembling Zippy from Rainbow, terrorising the law-abiding, church going townsfolk? Guess we'll never quite know the thinking behind this gem.

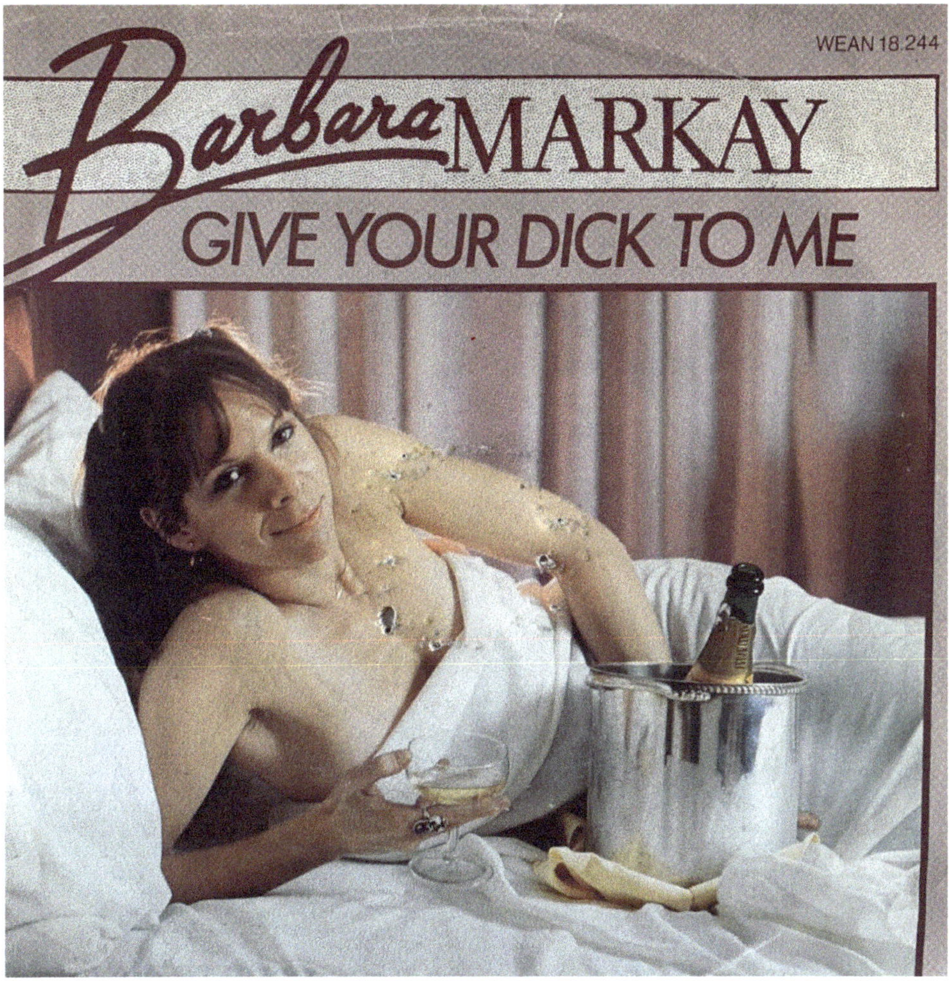

BARBARA MARKAY:
GIVE YOUR DICK TO ME

Well, old Babs certainly doesn't mince her words! Although classically trained, she rebelled by dumbing down and moving into the world of pop. I'm guessing it was the lure of the filthy yankee dollar. Markay released a string of sleazy pop tunes and collaborated with the likes of Michael Jackson, Eric Clapton and Quincy Jones, before entering her 'spiritual music phase'. Was this to make amends for past crimes? Maybe. "I was young, I needed the money", I hear her cry!

Her past canon during this period included classics such as 'It's All Right To Fuck All Night', 'Sessame Snatch' (sic), 'Vibrator Blues' and 'Hot Chocolate Cock'.

Go Babs.

KJELL KRAGHE OCH RICKE LÖW'S ORKESTER: VIND I SEGLEN

One of the joys of sailing is the ever changing seas and scenery, the challenges posed by the prevailing winds and the chance that one may spot a pod of dolphins frolicking in the distance, or the rare sea monster Kjell Kraghe on the horizon.

This scene of nautical nonsense was the Winner of the 1981 ugliest record cover in Sweden.

WAYNE KING:
THE SOUND OF WAYNE KING

Ever wondered what the sound of Wayne King is like? Geddit, eh? Put on this record and find out.

Some of the tracks give us a clue. A Time To Love, Come Closer To Me, and A Very Precious Love can all produce A Certain Smile.

As for the Baubles, Bangles and Beads… this must be Wayne King for the more adventurous amongst us. Say no more.

LJUDI:
LJUDI

Imagine Leicester on a Friday night at kicking out time following the zombie apocalypse. Add a flakka drug epidemic sweeping the city into the mix, and you have this nightmarish vision of hell on earth. And whilst the city burns, the saxophonist plays on with his cool notes – before being lamped by the local legged-up Leicester lager lout.

HERBERT ROTH:
MELODIEN

If you think Alan Partridge types are confined to Norfolk, England, then think again. Oddly, Alan Partridge translated into German is Alan Partridge. The same goes for Herbert Roth. We have more in common with our Teutonic neighbours than we care to admit.

TOMISLAV IVČIĆ:
GIRO D'ITALIA TALIJANSKA PLOČA 2

With his 'business on top, party around the back' mullet, walrus love moss moustache and all-white tracky, Tomislav resembles a Croatian version of the stereotypical Scouse 1980s man about town.

With his brothers Đani and Vedran also in the music business, one can imagine lots of 'Calm down' squabbles between the siblings, as they jockeyed for number one position in the family pop hierarchy.

KARTHAGO: SELF-TITLED

LEEEGGGIIIITTT!!!

Baba, the four tusked lazer firing elephant has gone ape shit, smashing the crap out of, er, plants. Steady on jumbo, you might need to eat that valuable foliage in an otherwise barren and erupting landscape. You got to think these things through first, big fella.

SAMSON:
SURVIVORS

With their bad rock and song titles on this album such as 'I Wish I was The Saddle Of A Schoolgirl's Bike', let's pray that Samson are not the future survivors of a post apocalyptic brave new world.

TERRE THAEMLITZ:
OH, NO! IT'S RUBATO

Identity politics activist and record label owner Terre Thaemlitz tackles complex themes of pan-sexuality, trans rights, race, gender fluidness and class consciousness through the prism of music, writings and public speaking.

Confused? This sleeve of his Jarvis Cocker-type head atop a potato floating above a desert road should help to clarify things.

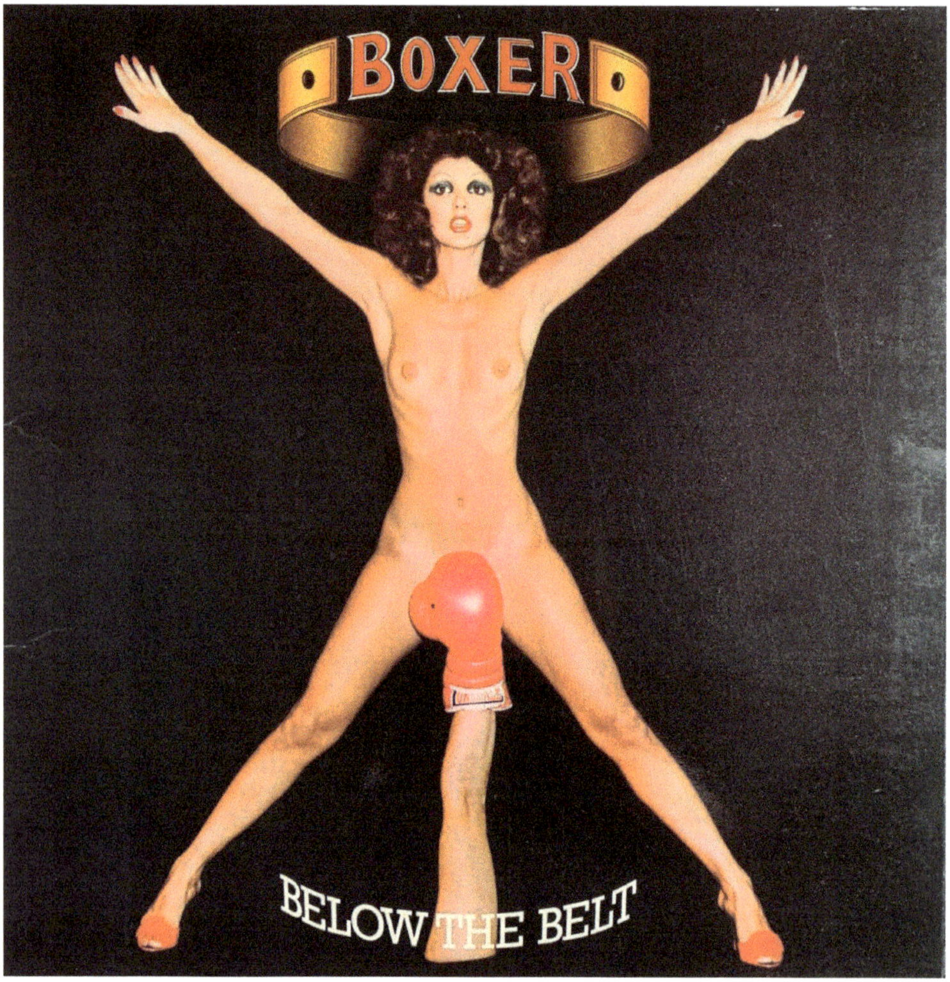

BOXER:
BELOW THE BELT

Released in 1975 from the ashes of Patto, Boxer's Below The Belt received more attention for its greasy sleeve than the actual music. The original pressings had a full frontal nude of Stephanie Marrian (the first page 3 model in The Sun) on the back cover, which was soon covered up on subsequent pressings. And the covering up here with a punch to the nether regions is probably worse than the original. The sleeve was completely redone for US sensibilities.

Sometimes, censorship can be forgiven.

DENNIS HAYWARD:
SEQUENCE TIME WITH DENNIS HAYWARD

You just know Dennis was one of the awkward 80s kids who spent his Saturdays in Rumbelows, playing with the Casio keyboards. There were scores of these nippers, pretending they were playing a perfect 'Camptown Races', when they had actually just hit the pre-set demo button. That or bashing the bossa nova pads, until the security guard turfed the scruffy urchins back out onto the street. Few of these kids actually managed to attain one of these expensive keyboards, but Dennis obviously did and took matters a step further. He released an album of himself cocking around with his bontempi.

John Shuttleworth, eat your heart out. DH is for real.

KATHI PRECHTL:
GRÜSSE AUS BAYERN (GREETINGS FROM BAVARIA)

Lordy, it's all going on in Bavaria. Kathi and Christiane are looking for love. Heidi and Hansl are in love, and so are Sepp and Eric, which seems very progressive for this 50 year old record. Maybe it's one big free-for-all. Ya, ya, das ist fantastisch!

Maybe the flowers in the window box are a dog whistle for Germans who are into this sort of malarkey, akin to the pampas grass clue found in UK swingers' front gardens. Or was that just an urban myth?

GYPSY QUEEN:
THE SNARL 'N STRIPES EP

GRRRRRRRRRR!!!

Gypsy Queen were fronted by Miami based flame-haired twins Paula and Pamela Mattioli. Hendrix aside, any band names or song titles mentioning Gypsy Woman / Lady / Queen etc are destined to be a bit tacky. As is putting tigers on your record sleeve, and dressing in big cat prints.

The feline connection doesn't end there, with rumours that the 'hair metal' twins provided lead vocals for the song Smelly Cat from the TV sitcom Friends.

LITTLE FEAT:
DOWN ON THE FARM

I know I used to have a crush on that sexy bunny from the Cadbury's Caramel advert back in the 80s, but this high class slutty duckie doesn't cut the mustard.

And what's with the riding crop on the table? I can't imagine it will be much use warding off the tiger in the background come dinner time.

MAC GAYDEN :
SKYBOAT

Gayden's achievements include part-writing 'Everlasting Love' and performing alongside Dylan, Simon & Garfunkel and Elvis. However, the story of his album Skyboat is one epic failure.

The nightmarishly chummy sleeve was supposed to represent the spiritual wonder of an Appalachian dream, as portrayed in the epic 10 minute end track 'Diamond Mandala'. Once released, as Gayden was from Nashville, promoters assumed it was yet another country record. It was therefore sent out exclusively to Country & Western radio stations, where it inevitably bombed.

One can imagine the good 'ole boys reaction upon playing this - even from the more broad minded Country AND Western brigade.

VARIOUS:
TIP FOR TOP

"Help, help... please stop... we are only little people... you're treading on us with your 1950s rockabilly dance moves."

BOBA:
OBRIŠI SUZE, DRAGA / KADA TE NEMA

Croatian casanova Boba, resplendent in purple attire, kipper tie, soft barnet and holding his crutch looks lovingly into your eyes, then whispers into your ear, "I want to make f@ck with you all night".

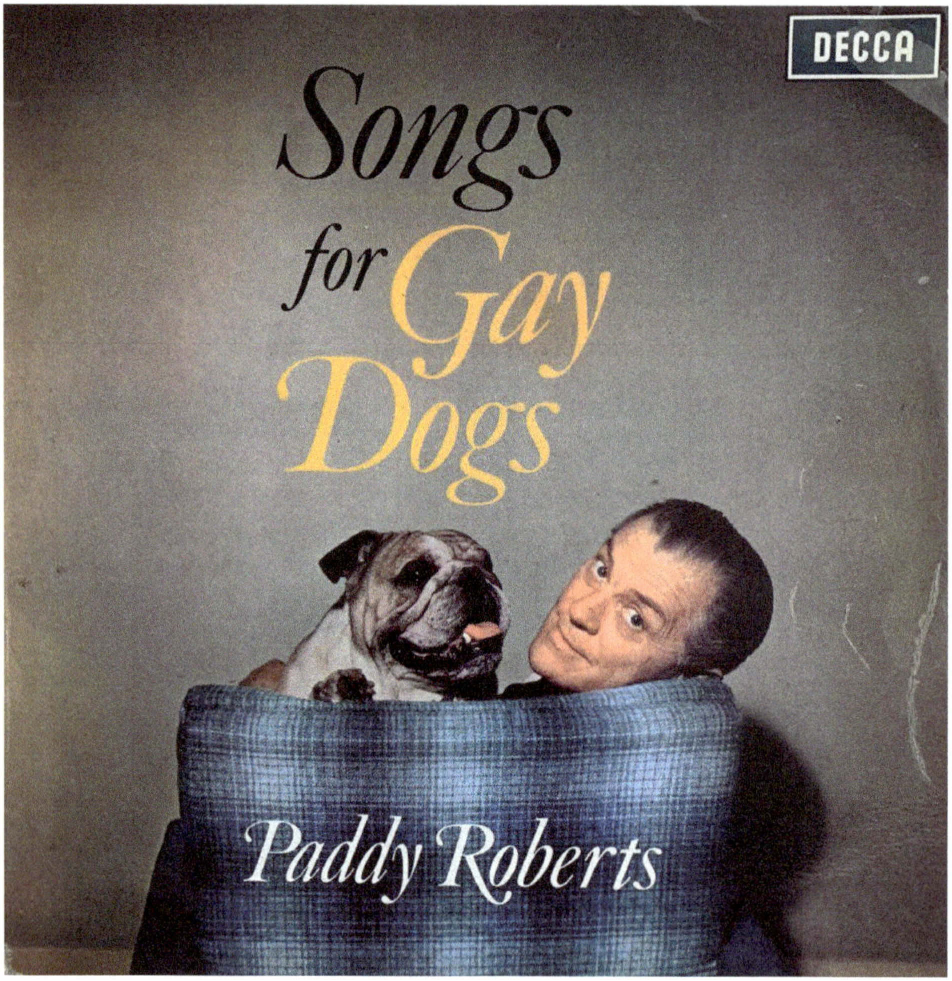

PADDY ROBERTS:
SONGS FOR GAY DOGS

At first glance, this looks like the least gay looking dog ever. But squint your eyes and imagine Butch here with a leather cap on his head and a studded collar around his neck.

Go get them limp wristed poodle doggies, Butch.

MASHINA VREMENI ROCK GROUP:
GOOD LUCK

With their fluffy bouffants, garishly bad suits with sleeves rolled up, shoulder pads and silk cravats, how apt that this Soviet band's name translates as 'Time Machine'. Even if we could send them back in time whence they came, I reckon their comrades would still laugh at them mercilessly. Bless their fluorescent cotton socks.

OMEGA 8:
CSILLAGOK ÚTJÁN

If we die and go to heaven, is this what it's like? Start behaving badly, folks.

DEAN REED:
A JEHO SVĚT

-"..and that's when I had my transcendental experience. It just wasn't flowing, I was flat out of creativity. So I decided to go for a walk in the woods. And that's when I came across The Tree of Wisdom."

-"The Tree of Wisdom? What the bloody 'ell are you going on about?"

-"It's a black tree with my face on it, but like dead big and that. It told me that I am the greatest singer/songwriter since Bob Dylan, so stop moping about and get cracking. And that's how I wrote this album."

-"Oh, right. Have you got that tenner you owe me?"

KINDEREN VERTELLEN MOPPEN AAN HARRY TOUW

'Ok guys, who farted?'

Now normally, if there was a chubby kid in the group, they would take one for the team and shoulder the blame. However, in their absence, we have to look at other suspects for the Crime of the Century.

I'm pointing the finger at the nipper on the far left. Yes you, laddo, in the pinkish top. He's not holding his nose and smirking very proudly to himself, basking in the warm afterglow of his outrageous behaviour.

MAYLEE TODD:
CHOOSE YOUR OWN ADVENTURE

Why not notch the bear slippers/onesie look up a level? This is what happens when your father is a Neil Diamond impersonator, your mother a creative visual artist and your grandfather an escapologist, with a habit of appearing on the front page of the local rag proclaiming his latest encounter with alien life forms.

LOVERBOY: GET LUCKY

The lion of the disco is on the prowl, peacocking in his best pulling pants. Who can resist this roister doister as he silkily moves in on his prey?

Funnily enough, the crossed fingers resemble the National Lottery's logo… .It Could Be You.

Fingers crossed it isn't.

SAVETA JOVANOVIĆ:
LAŽNO JE, LAŽNO, SVE ŠTO JE TVOJE

Us Brits have a long tradition of recounting tales of hirsute women met on the continent during our holidays in the 70s and 80s. An adventurous matey would hold court at the bar, and report back to an amused and horrified audience about these mythical hairy creatures, as if he had just been to a Victorian freak show. This sleeve proves that at least there was some truth in these instances of Euro-xenophobic bar room rabble-rousings.

THE INDIAN SELECTION PRESENTS JOHNNY BACHOE

Top tip for aspiring chutney musicians: When posing in front of a fake background, remember not to include the surrounding props in the finished photograph.

ENIO:
SAMP POJUPCI

Awkward dot com. Cue the other uncomfortable looking band members as the lecherous alpha male gang runner cops a feel of arse flesh.

Putting a mannequin in the frame doesn't make this sleeve highbrow or arty. It's still seedier than a pomegranate.

STEAM ROLLER:
CITY KIDS

Do you believe in unicorns? Alien life forms? Horses floating around space with sparkly manes and tails, and steam rollers for feet?

Nor do I.

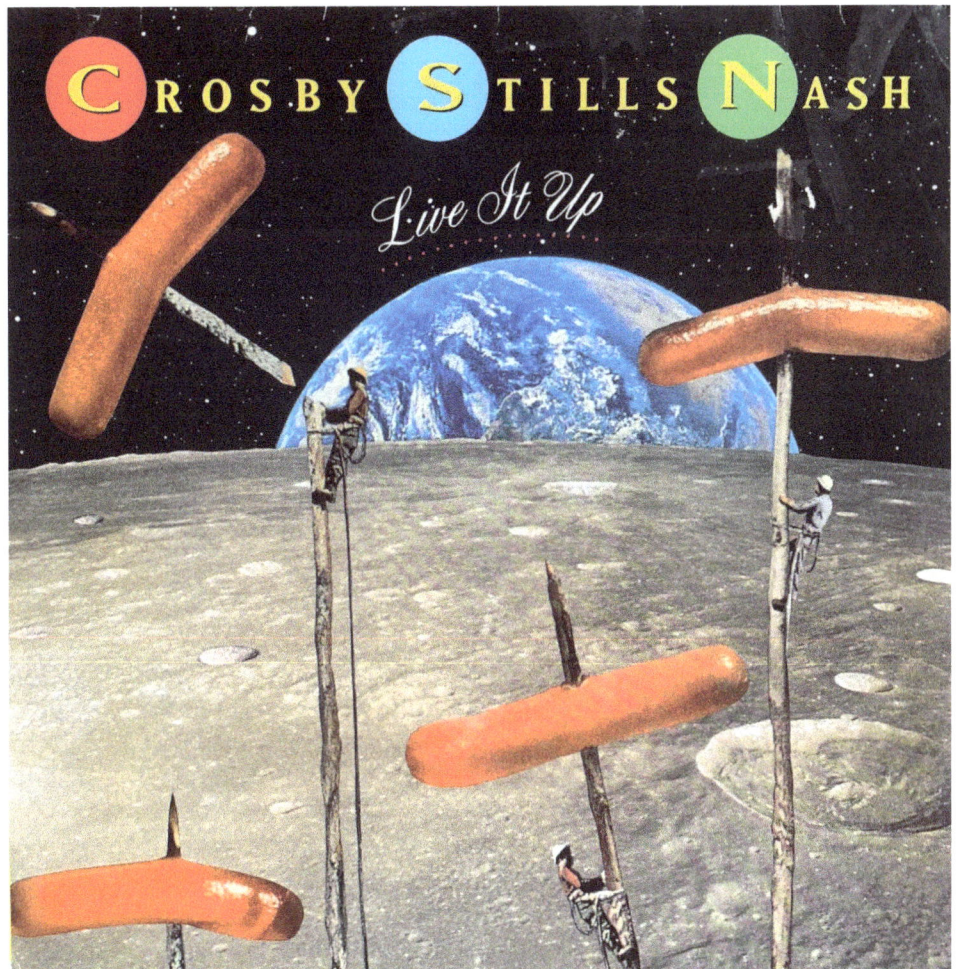

CROSBY, STILLS & NASH: LIVE IT UP

Dave Crosby of CSN had a colourful life, and how he is still alive as I write this is somewhat of a mystery. His drug and alcohol consumption was legendary, as was his love of firearms and brushes with the law, including time spent in the clink. One can only conclude therefore that it was Crosby (as opposed to the more sober Stills and Nash), that was behind this riddle of a sleeve during one of his potty crack pipe periods.

This sleeve proves that drugs don't always lead to an increase in creativity, kids.

FORMULA-1: QUEEN OF LIE

Check out this pound shop Iron Maiden effort from Russian bad rockers Formula-1. With its tacky fantasy artwork, poor grammar and song titles like 'Russian Eagle', 'American Nights' and 'Mad Driver', those crazy Ruskies really know how to rock... badly. It's 1992, and they still haven't heard that Jimi Hendrix is dead.

Queen Of Lie? King Of Naff, more like.

DAVID HASSELHOFF: NIGHT ROCKER

Where do you go after being Michael Knight, star and protagonist of the huge 80s TV show 'Knight Rider'? Why, you become the Night Rocker of course, belting out hairy-chested rock numbers in racy leathers. Other career highlights include starring in 'Baywatch', having a crab named after himself (The Hoff Crab) and being in the Guinness Book of Records for the highest ever reverse bungee jump. The Hoff is also a keen supporter of the Scottish football minnow, Partick Thistle F.C.

Bizarrely, the Hoffmeister still has a devoted following in Germany, and to a lesser extent, Switzerland. Make of that what you will.

#100

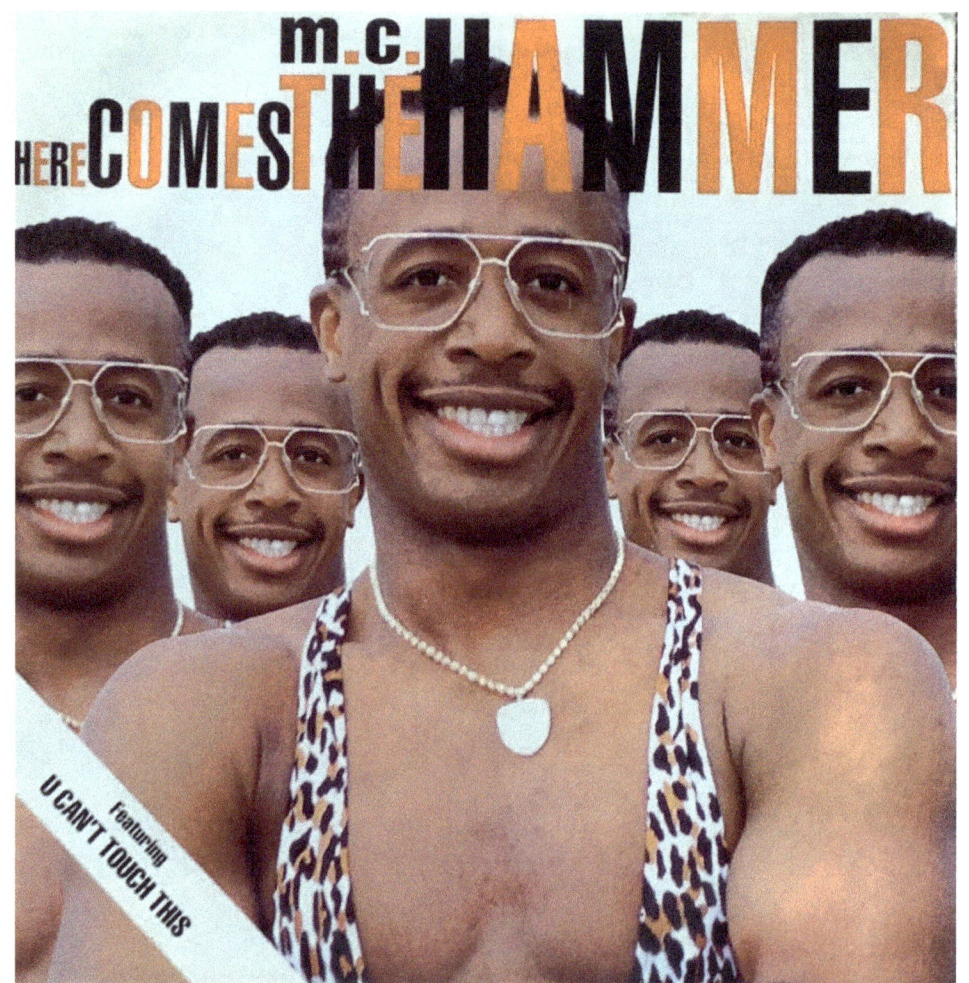

MC HAMMER:
HERE COMES THE HAMMER

What is five times worse than a bare-chested parachute pant wearing pop rapper in leopard prints grinning at you inanely? Yep, this record sleeve, like something straight from a nightmarish Aphex Twin video.

And it looks as if they are about to multiply further like Gremlins. They stare at you through the kitchen window as you wash up, smile at you as you pop down the shop for some milk and appear in your rear view mirror as you drive. Always with that grin, tormenting you slowly into insanity.

BUZZY LINHART:
PUSSYCATS CAN GO FAR

Buzzy Linhart is a musician.

Buzzy Linhart likes pussycats.

Buzzy Linhart secretly believes he also has feline traits.

Buzzy Linhart decides it is a good idea to express his therianthropic tendencies by way of sticking his permed head on a moggy's body for his latest record sleeve. And there he sits, looking very pleased with himself, grinning like a Cheshire cat.

ACKNOWLEDGEMENTS

All the record sleeves featured in this book are from the author's collection. Many thanks to all the artists who put out these wonderful sleeves.

Photography: Teresa Hulley

Cover Design: Michael Shepherd

Proofreading: Jane Ridley

Sharon Holloway of Reggie's Retro record store, Ventnor, Isle of Wight

A big shout out to Mum and Paul, Steve Gale, John Gleeson, Lenka Koprivova and Jeff Lewis for all your support.

The great DJs who play for the superb Flipside Society Radio Show.

Dedicated to Charlie Allen. Thank you for taking the time to walk with me.

Milton Keynes UK
Ingram Content Group UK Ltd.
UKHW050503050923
428034UK00004B/190